Aliens

15 Reasons to Believe

Conrad Bauer

All rights reserved. © Conrad Bauer and Maplewood Publishing No part of this publication or the information in it may be quoted from or reproduced in any form by means such as printing, scanning, photocopying, or otherwise without prior written permission of the copyright holder.

Efforts have been made to ensure that the information in this book is accurate and complete. However, the author and the publisher do not warrant the accuracy of the information, text, and graphics contained within the book due to the rapidly changing nature of science, research, known and unknown facts, and internet. The author and the publisher do not hold any responsibility for errors, omissions, or contrary interpretation of the subject matter herein. This book is presented solely for motivational and informational purposes only. References, if any, are provided for informational purposes only and do not constitute endorsement of any websites or other sources. Readers should be aware that the websites listed in this book, if any, may change.

ISBN: 9781674520537

Printed in the United States

MAPLEWOOD
— PUBLISHING —

Contents

Do You Believe? 1

The Moon: the Best Evidence for Aliens? 3

Ancient Aliens—Ancient Proof? 9

The Crash at Roswell, New Mexico 15

To Catch an Alien by the Hair: The Peter Khoury Story 21

Wow! Radio Signals of Alien Life? 25

The Skinwalker Ranch 29

Alien Implants 33

Cattle Mutilations 37

Crop Circles 41

Alien Abductions 43

Oumuamua 47

Exoplanets 49

Unexplained Disappearances 53

The Tunguska Incident 57

Disclosure or Disinformation? (You Blink and You Miss It!) ... 61

It's All in the Eye of the Beholder 71

Further Readings 73

Do You Believe?

Do you believe in aliens? If you do, then you're in good company. According to the latest polls and statistics, it has been projected that approximately half the people on the planet now believe that alien life exists in some form or other. This is a number that has grown exponentially over the past few decades. And while many of the more cynical analysts say this growth in belief has more to do with Hollywood science fiction films than anything to do with science, over the years a certain amount of evidence has begun to pile up.

The possibility that humanity is not alone in the cosmos has certainly become a popular topic of discussion, but even among those who believe, certain caveats separate the levels of that belief. There are many, for example, who firmly believe that aliens must exist *somewhere* in this incredibly vast universe. Even most scientists would now contend that out of the billions upon billions of stars, and the billions upon billions of planets that revolve around them, at least a few of them somewhere out there must have some sort of life on them.

Nowadays, the big question seems to be whether or not any of that life has ever been *here*. Some who insist that ET is fully capable of stopping by our little neck of the galactic woods are what you might call the "true believers." They can open their minds enough to consider all of those stories of UFOs buzzing through our atmosphere, picking up random hitchhikers, and messing with our cattle in the middle of the night.

Many aspects of the modern UFO phenomenon can sound completely absurd. But for some scientists, the very notion of aliens from other star systems are easily ping-ponging around the universe (and getting to our planet in the first place) is absurd in itself, since according to physics, nothing can travel faster than the speed of light.

And with that universal speed limit in place, it would seem that most potential alien star systems would be too far away for routine visits by the alien abductors we hear so much about. Even if they were coming from our closest star system, Alpha Centauri, at four light-years away, even at the speed of light, a round trip would take at least eight years to make. But supposing that no one can travel faster than light, even this is far from impossible.

For all we know, a civilization a thousand or so years ahead of us just might have warp drives, hyper-speed, and all manner of incredible, wormhole-busting equipment at their disposal that could turn our understanding of physics completely on its head. The truth is, when it comes to the capability of potential aliens, we really don't know. Just look at where we are today, versus technology a hundred years ago. Fifty, even.

Another civilization, given enough room to grow, just might find a shortcut through what we conventionally view as the constraints of space and time. They may have methods and abilities we haven't even dreamed of. As the great science fiction writer Isaac Asimov once put it, "Any sufficiently advanced technology is indistinguishable from magic."

Just because it blows our little minds, doesn't mean that another creature in this vast cosmos couldn't find a solution to the problem. Entertaining such possibilities, let's take a look at the evidence that aliens might exist, after all.

The Moon: the Best Evidence for Aliens?

At first glance, the idea of aliens inhabiting the moon probably seems like a patent absurdity cooked up in some pulp magazine from the 1930s. Back then, there were all kinds of imaginative tales telling of mountains, rivers, forests, and lakes covering the moon's surface. At one time, some even speculated that the moon's "Sea of Tranquility" actually was *a sea.*

But the Apollo missions confirmed that the moon was a dead, lifeless world with next to no atmosphere, no liquid water, and nothing even remotely resembling life. So how in the world could the moon be one of the best-kept secrets when it comes to evidence of aliens? Well, it's not so much that aliens live (or even once lived) on the moon – it's rather the idea that aliens may have somehow *built* the moon.

Built the moon? Sounds bizarre, right? Well, as it turns out, the moon is a very bizarre place. The moon, in fact, exhibits some of the greatest anomalies of the solar system, and these have yet to be adequately explained. The first of which is simply how the heck the moon came to exist in the first place. For a long time, scientists had speculated that the moon was a piece of the Earth that had broken off at some point in the distant past and remained captured in orbit.

This would make sense in many ways, since in the youth of our planet it was routinely bombarded with large asteroids that could feasibly have ripped off big chunks of the planet. Some, in fact, make the claim that perhaps the moon came out of the big gouge that now makes up the Pacific Ocean. But when the astronauts from Apollo brought back the first moon rocks, this theory was proven to be wrong.

Why? To the shock of the scientific world, the Apollo astronauts discovered that the moon was actually *older than the Earth!* One moon rock was found to be over 700 million years older than the oldest rocks on Earth. If the stuff the moon was made of was in existence before the Earth, then where in the heck was the moon hanging out before the Earth was formed?

It was these findings that led some to consider that while the moon could not have come from the Earth, perhaps it was just an elder remnant of debris from the formation of our solar system, which eventually made its way around the still forming, early Earth. But as closer scrutiny was turned upon the moon and this particular problem, the inherent difficulty of this new explanation was made clear.

First of all, by most estimates, the moon seems too large to have been so seamlessly locked into Earth's orbit. If Earth was pulling in such a large body, the more likely outcome would have been for that object to get pulled down onto Earth's surface, creating a colossal explosion as the two objects collided. But instead, the moon was pulled into a perfect, circular orbit, in which the moon is not only firmly locked in place, but also completely immobile, with one side perpetually showing itself to the Earth, while the other continually faces outward.

The moon does not rotate; we only see one side of it from our vantage point on Earth, with the so-called "dark side" of the moon always pointing away from us. This is a peculiar coincidence and the moon is said to be the only known "natural satellite" to be in such a condition. But perhaps the most stunning coincidence of the moon's orbit is that it is in just the right position – and just the right distance from both the Earth and the sun – to create the spectacular event that we know of down here on Earth as a "total lunar eclipse."

Most take it for granted, but the fact that the moon, which is considerably smaller than the sun, happens to be positioned just the right distance from Earth so that it appears to be approximately the same size when we look up into the sky. It is this precise distancing that allows the moon – from our vantage point down here – to cross over and appear to completely cover the sun in an eclipse.

Just to bring home how bizarre this situation truly is, just think about it: the moon is not even half as big as the Earth, and the sun is humongous, with a diameter of 864,938 miles. About 110 planet Earths easily could fit inside the sun. The sun, of course, only appears the size it is because it's about 93 million miles away. The fact that the moon happens to be just the right size (and just the right distance from Earth) to create a total eclipse is mind-boggling – and no other planet in our solar system is blessed with such a coincidence.

That is, of course, if it is a coincidence at all. Those who are inclined to be religious in contemplating this rare anomaly might point to God. They would say that this was a sign of a creator's divine hand in creation. Others, however, wonder if something else might be afoot. If the moon wasn't put in place by natural or divine forces, perhaps it was placed there by extraterrestrial forces.

The moon is indeed an oddity, but to say that it was somehow dropped off by aliens? That's crazy talk, right?

Well, the astronauts from the Apollo missions might hesitate to agree with that completely, because they came to the conclusion that the moon appears to be, if not completely hollow, at least semi-hollow.

The moon, rather than having a dense, heavy core in the center, has been found to instead have dense, heavy materials right on the surface, making the outer layer more like a metal hull than a soft crust. This is strange, but perhaps the most startling indication of the moon potentially being hollow occurred on the 20th of November, 1969, when the Apollo crew returned to their command ship and dropped their staging onto the moon's surface.

Seismic equipment onboard the ship recorded the impact as it happened, and to the astonishment of the watching astronauts, the readings indicated that upon being struck, the moon reverberated like a bell for over an hour. Only a hollow moon would do such a thing. It was in light of some of these findings that a couple of Russian scientists, Alexander Scherbakov and Mikhail Vasin, put forth the notion that the moon was actually an alien-engineered spacecraft of some sort, one that was parked in the moon's orbit.

It sounds pretty bizarre, doesn't it? But these Russian researchers maintained that a sufficiently advanced alien civilization would be capable of hollowing out a small planetoid and converting it into an interstellar craft. According to them, this would be done using huge machines to melt away the inside of the space rock and spew its contents back out onto the surface, creating a hard outside covering and a hollow interior.

Inside, complex interior components of the structure would be built. This world-sized craft was then supposedly launched and sent on a flight path that eventually led to Earth's orbit. Vasin and Scherbakov realized just how wild their theory sounds, but nevertheless, they held fast to their findings.

Scherbakov declared, "Abandoning the traditional paths of 'common sense', we have plunged into what may at first sight seem to be unbridled and irresponsible fantasy. But the more minutely we go into all the information gathered by man about the Moon, the more we are convinced that there is not a single fact to rule out our supposition. Not only that, but many things so far considered to be lunar enigmas are explainable in the light of the new hypothesis."

In other words, as crazy as this lunatic lunar theory may sound, it is the only hypothesis that actually answers all of the lingering questions about why the moon is so unusual. So, what are the odds? Did aliens have something to do with the moon? Perhaps the evidence of their existence is looking us right in the face on any given moonlit night of the week.

Ancient Aliens—Ancient Proof?

The notion that ancient extraterrestrial visitors came to Earth in some distant, primordial past has certainly picked up a lot of steam in recent years, with everything from the pyramids to the moon imagined to be alien constructs. Many have credited Swiss writer Erich Von Daniken with launching the original concept through his seminal work "Chariots of the Gods."

However, it was actually the late, great astronomer Carl Sagan who first went on record proposing the theory in depth. He had discussed the idea at length in the early 1960s, several years prior to Von Daniken. In a research paper that was actually funded by a NASA research grant, he pointed out certain oddities in ancient human civilizations which seemed to point to extraterrestrial visitors.

Strangely, even though Sagan birthed the concept, after coming up with it he spent most of his life discrediting it! He developed a passionate dislike of Von Daniken and the growing popularity of what was then called the "ancient astronaut theory," and attempted to debunk it whenever he could. The strange about-face Carl Sagan made on this matter has led some conspiracy theorists to believe that there was more to this than Sagan simply changing his mind. Some believe that when he was on NASA's payroll, his superiors encouraged him to become a debunker. It is furthermore alleged that these efforts increased when NASA began exploring solar system bodies such as the moon and Mars.

At any rate, Sagan introduced the idea and Von Daniken and others later made it popular with the public. The concept of ancient astronauts, or as they are better known today, "ancient aliens," has taken the world by storm. Countless books, TV programs, and documentaries have endlessly covered the topic, with some seeming more credible than others.

Some theorists are criticized for seeing aliens around every archeological corner, while others have been careful to focus on just a few key anomalies found around the globe. While we don't have the time or luxury to discuss them all, here in this chapter we will focus on some of the most compelling possible indications of past visitation.

Ancient Mesopotamia

The ancient Mesopotamian civilization is rightfully prefaced with the word "ancient." Dating back 10,000 years, it was within this early civilization that the first written records were created. Crafted by the Sumerians of Mesopotamia in 3500 BC, the written text is known as "cuneiform" and for the most part contains mundane facts about daily Sumerian life. Much of it simply records who owned what cattle, and who owed what bushel of wheat. But in the midst of these daily dealings, the ancient Sumerians of Mesopotamia had quite a story to tell. For it was the ancient Sumerian scribes who spoke of beings called the "Anunnaki" descending down onto the Earth from the stars and teaching them the rudiments of civilization.

Just a good story, right? Well, one would assume that this was all just mythology – except that some of the specific details conveyed in the account contain information that the ancient Sumerians should have had no way of knowing. The most glaring revelation is the fact that these ancient people had a complete working knowledge of the solar system. Thousands of years before a telescope was even imagined, the Sumerians somehow knew all of the planets, including their approximate size and their distance from the sun. In order to understand just how incredibly advanced the Sumerians' knowledge of these things was, just consider that until Christopher Columbus sailed in 1492, most people thought the Earth was a flat place and the sole center of creation, around which the sun, moon, and stars revolved. Yet somehow, in 3500 BC, about 5000 years prior to Columbus, the Sumerians knew that the Earth was round and that it revolved around a star we call the sun. They knew about all the other planets of the solar system, including greatly detailed depictions of the outer planets Uranus and Neptune, the latter of which the rest of the world wouldn't even know about until 1846!

As mentioned, the Sumerians didn't have access to even basic telescopes, so how did they know these things? Well, according to the Sumerians, they knew it because it was what the Anunnaki told them! The Sumerians' clay tablets also mention that the Anunnaki teachers came to Earth 400,000 years ago and altered human genetics. The Sumerian text goes into great detail about genetic material being spliced together and cooked up in what seems to be a description of laboratory equipment. Furthermore, there is early Mesopotamian artwork depicting the Anunnaki holding what do indeed look like long glass tubes, in what are apparently corresponding detailed scenes from this strange narrative. Just to be clear, the text does not say that the Anunnaki created humans, it just contends that they genetically manipulated and engineered the human race that was already here. Either the Sumerians were very imaginative, or there is a whole unknown epoch of human history that we know very little about.

Egypt's Pyramids

The pyramids of Egypt have always held a fascination for humanity. These megastructures are one of the few artificial constructs that can actually be seen from outer space – and some alien theorists believe that this is so for a reason. According to them, ancient aliens either built or helped build these colossal structures. Some find this notion offensive (whether they think it feasible or not) because they claim that it does a disservice to the ancient people of Egypt to contend that they were not capable of building the pyramids on their own. However, there are native Egyptian legends that assert the same thing, stating that "sky gods" came down in their "sky boats" and began the work of building the pyramids and the sphinx. Known as the legend of "Zep Tepi" or the "First Time," this account contends that tens of thousands of years ago, humanity was guided by celestial entities. The Egyptians referred to them as gods, but through the lens of ancient astronaut theory, they would be perceived as extraterrestrials. These beings are said to have served as guides and even direct rulers in Egypt during the time of Zep Tepi. Eventually, however, they were said to have handed power over to lesser so-called demigods that were half human, half god, or as the ancient astronaut theory would contend, half human, half alien.

Such fanciful tales have led ancient astronaut theorists to seize upon the fact that many of the ancient leaders of Egypt were depicted in what many would say was an unusual fashion. They were often made out to be extremely skinny, tall figures, with large, oblong heads which were usually partially concealed in the conical ceremonial headdress that Egyptian rulers wore.

But back to the pyramids—if they were made by aliens, why? What were they for? The theories here really run the gamut, with some of the more exotic claiming that the pyramids were nuclear reactors, or that they were communication antennas to beam messages back to other solar systems, or even that they were some sort of geological transformers that aliens used to help modify, or even terraform Earth's early environment.

But even if all of these legends and theories are utter nonsense, no one has ever managed to explain just how the pyramids were built. During a time even before the invention of the wheel, the fact of the pyramids' very existence presents a great mystery. If aliens were not involved, it is evident that the ancient Egyptians did have capabilities that we still find hard to comprehend.

The Nazca Lines of Peru

The Nazca Lines of Peru are sometimes referred to as the crop circles of the ancient world. This is due to their similarity to crop circles, as both are strange designs etched into the environment that can be seen from several miles up. But crop circles are temporary; they last for a season and then are grown over with new wheat, corn, or whatever else grows there. The Nazca lines, however, have been stretched across several miles of Peruvian desert for thousands of years, remaining relatively undisturbed. They were discovered only fairly recently, first sighted by modern eyes in 1937 when a pilot flew over the region. This, and many more aspects of the lines, has led many to conclude that they were indeed meant to be seen from the air – they simply are not comprehensible from the ground. But once man had mastered flight, and the first planes started flying overhead, the long lines etched in the ground that make up the geometric patterns and images were easily recognizable. The obvious question is, why would a people who lived long before airplanes were invented construct elaborate geoglyphs that could only be seen from the air? This, of course, is the clincher when it comes to the idea of aliens being somehow responsible for the Nazca lines. Although even ancient astronaut theorists can't claim to know for sure, some have speculated that perhaps aliens had visited the region, and the people longing for the return of the powerful beings who had befriended them drew the huge images on the ground in an effort to say "Here we are! Come back!" Along with animal shapes and geometric designs, one of them depicts a humanoid figure waving up at the sky, almost as if it were indeed beckoning for someone, or something, to make a return appearance.

The Mayan Civilization

Now that all the 2012 hype is behind us, we can take a conclusive look at the role the Mayan Civilization played in the formation of world culture. In particular, how it managed to raise the eyebrows of ancient astronaut theorists. The Mayans, just like the Sumerians and the Egyptians, have an origin story that claims they were founded by a being that came down from the sky. For the Mayans, their extraterrestrial founder was a creature they called Quetzalcoatl. Quetzalcoatl was the "feathered serpent god" of the Mayans who allegedly came down from the stars to help teach them the rudiments of civilization as well as astronomy and advanced mathematics. The Mayans revered their benefactor and when he left, they longed for his return – a return that they predicted would occur in the year 2012.

Now that we are pushing into the early 2020s, it is fairly obvious that Quetzalcoatl has yet to arrive. But looking at the Mayan civilization, there are still a lot of bizarre anomalies that suggest the possibility of an extraterrestrial visitation in the past. For example, inside the Mayan tomb complex in Palenque, a depiction of the Mayan ruler Pakal has been discovered in which he is operating what can only be described as some sort of craft. Pakal is pictured looking determinedly straight ahead while his hands are busy at the controls. Flames shoot out the back of the vehicle, giving the whole thing the appearance of a rocket ship in operation.

The other oddity about the Mayans that can't be overlooked is the fact of their inexplicable, sudden, and seemingly random disappearance. By the year 900, this great Mesoamerican civilization vanished without a trace. They did not succumb to famine, disease, or war; they seem to have simply quietly wandered away from their great cities for no apparent reason. By the time of the Europeans' arrival in the 1500s, although explorers were able to find the impressive Mayan cities that were left behind, they were completely empty and devoid of life. This has led some to theorize that perhaps Quetzalcoatl and his celestial cohorts did return after all; he just came to collect his followers a little bit earlier than anticipated.

The Crash at Roswell, New Mexico

The alleged crash at Roswell, New Mexico has been rehashed for several decades now – so much so that some may feel the urge to roll their eyes at its mere mention. But when it comes to potential evidence of alien visitation, the saga of Roswell cannot be overlooked. Although the supposed evidence this case provides is largely anecdotal in nature, the sheer volume of accounts provides us with the heftiest of all extraterrestrial circumstantial evidence.

So, let's briefly run through the series of events as they are said to have occurred. Around July 1st, 1947, unknown objects began to appear on radar in New Mexico. The U.S. army had no explanation for the craft and began carefully monitoring them. Then on July 2nd, a glowing object was sighted in the sky.

Attempts were made by military fighters to intercept the intruder, but these were unsuccessful. By July 4th it was all over; the object had disappeared from radar. On July 5th, a local rancher named Mac Brazel allegedly stumbled across a debris field nearly a mile long scattered across his property. At the same time, a soil conservation engineer by the name of Grady L. Barnett allegedly stumbled upon what was apparently the main wreckage of the craft.

While Brazel only had to deal with a ton of indistinct debris, Barnett allegedly saw the main command module of the craft half submerged in the desert sands. Some would later suggest that what Barnett encountered was really an emergency ejection pod that was released before the main ship came down, but if that was true, it failed to save the lives of the occupants.

Barnett claimed he found several corpses that were decidedly not human, and said that as startled as he was, he didn't have much time to process what he was seeing because just moments later, U.S. military personnel converged on the scene in a convoy of trucks and ordered him to leave the area.

Brazel, meanwhile, couldn't make heads or tails of what was strewn across his ranch, and growing alarmed, paid a visit to the local sheriff, who upon hearing of the crashed debris instructed him to get in touch with the local military base. As soon as Brazel notified the military of what he had, just like they did at the other alleged crash site, they quickly shut down the area to outside traffic.

Despite this rush to control access, on July 8th the army sent out a press release bluntly stating that they had captured a "flying disc" which had crashed near Roswell, New Mexico. The newspapers then immediately began running stories that the army was in possession of a "flying saucer" – a term that had been coined earlier that year when the first major UFO wave hit the nation.

Someone somewhere must not have liked this revelation, because within hours the military was doing an about-face and telling the media that the "excitement was not justified." They then retracted the story of the disc, claiming that it was just a weather balloon. To dispel rumors, they then allowed photographers to come to the office of Brigadier General Roger Ramey, who had been charged with handling the incident, where the man was subsequently photographed with debris from a weather balloon.

Years later, many would claim that the weather balloon material was planted after the fact in a clumsy sleight of hand orchestrated just to shut people up. The newspaper photographers dutifully took pictures of Ramey posing with the aluminum foil radar reflector of a weather balloon and the story was over...or at least the U.S. army hoped it was.

But interestingly, even in those canned photos of Ramey posing with the weather balloon, a strange anomaly was present that wouldn't be noticed until several years later. During the time of the incident, General Ramey was a busy man rushing to put out this fire or that, and it seems that he was being rushed around to such an extent that he didn't even have time to put away his official paperwork. Clutched in his hand right there in the photograph is what appears to be a top-secret piece of correspondence. It was only with the advent of computerized enhancement that the crumpled paper was magnified to reveal part of what was written on it. Even with the aforementioned enhancements not everything is entirely visible, but there is enough discernible text on the page to be of interest – in particular, the words, "victims of the wreck" and "aviators in the disc."

Just what wreck and what disc is this memo talking about? It is rather strange that during a press conference in which Ramey was aggressively asserting to the media that there was no captured disc, he was holding a piece of paper in his hand that was talking about the victims of a wreck – the aviators in the disc!

But nevertheless, whatever may have happened, the Roswell incident was indeed effectively hushed up for the next few decades. It wasn't until 1978, when UFO researcher Stanton Friedman began to speak with key people involved (such as Major Jesse Marcel, who had personally overseen the collection of some of the wreckage) that a quite different story began to emerge.

Since then, hundreds of additional witnesses, ranging from hospital staff who allegedly saw dead aliens to a funeral director ordered to provide several child-sized caskets, have come forward with their accounts of strange happenings in Roswell, New Mexico during the summer of 1947.

Meanwhile, the government has changed its official version of what happened in Roswell a few times. Initially, they claimed it was a simple weather balloon, but that story changed in the early 1990s when the Pentagon issued a new report in which it admitted the weather balloon story was a lie but insisted that it was only used as a cover story to prevent a secret experiment called "Project Mogul" from being compromised. Allegedly, the reason for the secrecy was that Mogul involved high altitude balloons that were used to detect potential nuclear explosions from America's Cold War nemesis of the time, the Soviet Union. But the behavior of the U.S. military after the crash seems much different than would be expected if this was a routine, albeit secret, experiment.

According to UFO researcher Jim Mars, several Mogul balloons had been launched, and most of the time, the military never even bothered to retrieve them. This lax behavior was certainly at odds with the reaction to whatever crashed in Roswell, since the area was immediately cordoned off and civilians were threatened and told to leave and never speak a word of what they had seen.

Oh, and what about those alien bodies? According to this explanation, Mogul used test dummies. The insinuation was that witnesses saw burned, disfigured mannequins in the desert rather than dead extraterrestrials.

Nevertheless, witnesses couldn't be kept quiet forever, and testimony continued to leak out. Perhaps one of the most thought-provoking testimonies came from Lieutenant Colonel Philip J. Corso. In 1997, when Mr. Corso was terminally ill with cancer, he dropped a whole new bombshell on the Roswell story. Corso, with the help of ufologist William Birns, wrote a book called *The Day After Roswell*.

In this text, he details work that he was personally involved in after the Roswell crash. His duties supposedly involved assessing recovered alien tech from the crash and then organizing a team of experts to back-engineer the recovered alien technology. According to Corso's book, although they were unable to replicate the craft itself, certain alien components were directly responsible for breakthroughs in other fields.

For example, Corso alleged that modern fiber optics and computer chips were all developed using tech recovered from the Roswell crash. So, if we are to believe Corso's testimony, although it was beyond the capabilities of military engineers to build their own flying saucer, we can thank space aliens for our laptops and the nifty smartphones that we've all come to know and love!

The UFO community, meanwhile, seems evenly split about Corso. There were those who really wanted to believe what he said, but others remained skeptical. Some even wondered if he was a disinformation agent of the government, spreading false tales to muddy the waters. Again, without any hard evidence to support his claims, all we really have is Colonel Corso's testimony.

If he were a witness, probably the strongest endorsement of his statement would be the fact that it was the last thing he did. Colonel Corso passed away shortly after his revelatory book came out. He kept his silence for several decades and only came forward when he knew his life was coming to an end. Many would find it hard to believe that someone with a terminal illness would choose to tell a big fat lie right before they died. Due to their clarifying nature, deathbed confessions are typically viewed as highly credible. And Corso's revelations are essentially that: a bombshell of a Roswell deathbed confession. Corso in particular has come to embody the Roswell case in general, in the sense that even though there is no smoking gun to show any of it actually happened, there is certainly a whole lot of compelling testimony that *something* did.

To Catch an Alien by the Hair: The Peter Khoury Story

Most stories of alien encounters are supported by absolutely no evidence, leading those who hear them with nothing but anecdotal tales and testimony with which to decide whether they believe the story or not. But the case of Peter Khoury is different because he allegedly managed to literally catch an alien by the hair.

Khoury claims to have experienced encounters with aliens on multiple occasions, with instances involving the classic gray aliens as well as strange gnomish blue-skinned creatures dressed in hooded cloaks. His supposed encounters were diverse and wide-ranging. But the incident that would gain him the most notoriety wouldn't involve little gray or blue men, but rather a couple of human-like – yet not quite so human – women.

The incident occurred in 1992, after Koury briefly dozed off to sleep. In the strange story that unfolded, he claimed he was suddenly jolted awake when he felt someone pressing down on the bed. His wife was gone at the time and he was the only person home. He opened his eyes, and still half asleep, he couldn't believe what he was seeing: two strange-looking women. One had black hair and what he recalled to be an "Asian" appearance and another, who looked more Scandinavian in her makeup, with Khoury stating that she had golden blond hair going halfway down her back.

According to Khoury, both women were naked and sitting at the foot of his bed. Khoury was obviously shocked at the intrusion and knew that he was in the grip of something very strange indeed. Although the women looked primarily human, their features were off in a way that told him that they were not *entirely* human. Khoury claims that their faces seemed too chiseled, with very high cheekbones and long faces, elfish noses, and eyes that were wide set and bigger than they should have been.

According to Khoury, before he could process events any further, the blonde woman leaned toward him, cupped the back of his head, and pulled his face down into her breasts. The bewildered Khoury tried to pull back, but feeling weak and in a daze, he couldn't quite break free. This strange woman also seemed unusually strong, and the more he struggled, the tighter her grip became.

She was soon pressing his face into her chest so hard that Khoury was having trouble breathing. In an absolute panic, he did the only thing he felt he could do, he bit down on one of her nipples. Shockingly, Khoury alleges he managed to tear away a piece of her nipple. After this, the woman immediately let Khoury go, but she didn't seem to be in any pain.

Oddly, she just seemed confused. Khoury claims that he received a sort of telepathic impression from her that basically went along the lines of, "This isn't supposed to happen. You've done this wrong." Khoury, catching his breath, then accidentally swallowed the small piece of flesh he had bit off and was immediately sent into a coughing spasm.

It was while he was in the midst of his coughing that the two women disappeared. They were simply there one moment and then were gone the next. According to Khoury, as soon as the beings vanished, it was as if a spell had been broken and he was once again in full control of his senses. He was then able to get up out of bed and walk to the bathroom.

He began to throw up. To his horror, he found that whatever the material was that he had bitten off and swallowed, it seemed to be stuck in his throat and was causing him to be violently ill. He gagged and choked but the material wouldn't come out. Finally, he went to the kitchen and drank a lot of water until he was sure he had flushed the substance down.

Whatever the material was, it could have served as a form of physical evidence but Khoury never retrieved it. But this wasn't the end of the story, because after drinking his water he went to the bathroom to relieve himself, and found wrapped around his penis a long hair that he knew was not his own.

What he did next might seem a little odd, but considering the circumstances, he knew that there was something unusual about the artifact. He took the hair, sealed it up in a plastic bag, and stored it away. It was this piece of alleged alien evidence that found its way into the hands of UFO researcher Bill Chalker. Bill had the material sent off to a lab and he and everyone else involved were quite surprised at what they found.

Under the microscope, it was discovered that the hair's genetic makeup was indeed highly unusual. Even at first glance it was strange, since it was extremely thin and nearly translucent, indicating that it lacked any pigment whatsoever.

And once the DNA was extracted, things became even stranger. The DNA is said to have come back as an extremely rare ethnic lineage known as the "Chinese Mongoloid type." Although it couldn't be heralded as an outright alien hair, it contained some of the rarest DNA groupings on the planet. Making it even more unusual was that this DNA group almost always had black hair, yet this strand of hair was blonde. The DNA type was so rare that only a handful of people on the planet would have this specific sequence, and none of them would have had naturally blonde hair.

After these findings on the hair's shaft, the forensics team then went on to test the root and discovered even more oddities. It was found that the hair contained a strand of DNA that was particularly resistant to viruses; it was missing a couple of genes that most humans have for a certain protein called CCR5. The scientists in the lab immediately recognized the significance of this, since those who lack these proteins are among the rare few who are immune to contracting HIV/AIDS.

This would make one wonder, of course, if such a thing was indeed by design. Many researchers in the field contend that the two entities Peter Khoury encountered were alien/human hybrids tasked with breeding with full-blooded human males to create more hybrids. If this were the case, and such creatures were routinely sent to breed with random humans, providing them with an automatic immunity to the worst of sexually transmitted diseases would seem like a logical safeguard.

While the hair provided by Peter Khoury is not necessarily a smoking gun proof of aliens, with the slew of anomalies present in its makeup it trends very heavily in that direction. And even though the testing is time consuming and expensive, Bill Chalker hopes to perform even more exhaustive tests that just might produce the kind of definitive evidence everyone is looking for in this elusive field.

Wow! Radio Signals of Alien Life?

Does ET phone home? Well, what about phoning us? For many years now, scientists have maintained that radio signals between the stars would be the most probable way that two civilizations might send messages to each other. This idea was first presented in the 1960s, when a couple of physicists from Cornell University, Giuseppe Cocconi and Philip Morrison, conducted a thought experiment on how aliens might try to reach out and ring up planet Earth.

They determined that if we were looking for messages from extraterrestrials, then we should be looking for radio signals. They maintained that although radio was a technology that any advanced extraterrestrial civilization would most likely learn very early on, radio would continue to be a mainstay because of its nature. Radio waves are powerful, easy to create, and can easily cover long distances between stars.

The two scientists also conjectured that aliens would most likely use a very specific bandwidth (1420 megahertz, because it is the frequency of hydrogen, the most abundant element) and recommended looking in that particular range. So, when radio astronomer Jerry Ehman at the Big Ear telescope at Ohio State University turned his radio telescope toward the constellation of Sagittarius to search for signals in the recommended range, he was shocked to receive a powerful transmission almost as soon as he pointed the telescope in that direction.

He was so shocked that he wrote the word "Wow!" in big, red letters on the computer printout that accompanied the reception of the transmission. But as incredible as the radio signal was, like a powerful beacon shined into the vast darkness of space, try as Ehman might, he could never pick up the signal again. The original signal lasted a couple of minutes before suddenly cutting off, and then there was nothing.

He repeatedly pointed the radio antenna in the direction that had picked up the Wow! signal but there was now simply nothing there. This led many to speculate early on that whatever was sending out the radio signal was not stationary, but moving very rapidly. Although there is no concrete proof of this, SETI's (Search for Extraterrestrial Intelligence) Seth Shothstack has postulated that perhaps it was some sort of transmission between two interstellar craft in deep space that had been intercepted.

But in 2016, a much more cautious explanation was proffered to the mystery of the Wow! signal when an astronomy professor named Antonio Paris offered an alternative view. According to Paris, the Wow! signal wasn't a rapid salvo from aliens but a fast burst from a distant comet. Those not familiar with the concept might wonder, comets emit radio signals?

Yes, under certain conditions, the hydrogen gas of comets can indeed emit radio frequencies. Hydrogen gas is released when the ice that coats comets is melted by the ultraviolet light of suns. This release of vapor from melted ice is what creates a comet's tail, which can extend a million miles in length. According to this theory, passing comets could generate a fast and powerful radio burst that could explain the signal.

Paris went so far as to point out that two comets did indeed pass through the area of space Ehman was targeting that day. Ehman and many others, however, say "not so fast." They object to this theory on the grounds that a comet's release of hydrogen would not be sufficient to create as powerful a signal as the Wow! signal was. Ehman asserts that the two comets Paris speaks of would have sent out two separate spikes on his readout, not just one fine-tuned burst.

If comets could trip off radio telescopes so easily, telescopes all over the world would be receiving Wow! signals on a daily basis. Additionally, a signal from a comet should repeat; even a comet passing fast should be detected more than once, but with the Wow! signal this simply wasn't the case.

As it stands, Ehman's Wow! signal from 1977 is still one of a kind; there has never been another transmission from deep space like it.

The Wow! signal seemed to have been turned on and quickly turned off in such a rapid manner that it defies any known natural phenomenon. However, extraterrestrial true believers just might be in luck with this one, because almost as soon as Paris put his theory out, most experts tended to agree with Jerry Eman that there was no way passing comets could have created something so unique.

So, in many ways, as we enter into the new decade of the 2020s, the Wow! Signal of 1977 is right back where it started. Experts are not saying that they are 100% sure it came from aliens; but it very well could be from other beings far away.

The Skinwalker Ranch

Not everyone has heard of the Skinwalker Ranch (also known as the Sherman Ranch), but it is alleged to be one of the preeminent paranormal hotspots on the planet. Located in a remote corner of Utah, it has a history of all sorts of strange happenings. The area has been rife with perceived paranormal activity for hundreds of years, with legends dating back to early Native American settlements.

Native American lore has provided this appellation; the skinwalker is an entity of Navajo lore that is said to be a shape-shifter and have a whole host of paranormal abilities. But what does all of this hocus pocus have to do with aliens? The convergence began when aerospace engineer, founder of Bigelow Aerospace, and avowed UFO buff Robert Bigelow purchased the ranch from its previous owners.

The previous tenants had become frightened by the things that were happening on the property. During their time on the ranch, they had witnessed cattle mutilations, UFOs, and even more traditional skin-walker manifestations taking place. If most people heard that a house or piece of land was seemingly haunted by bizarre interdimensional entities it would be a deal breaker, but wealthy tycoon Robert Bigelow saw it as a prime location to make an investment!

Bigelow purchased the ranch with the intent of conducting an exhaustive study of the paranormal activity that was happening. He stationed a team of scientists to work around the clock gathering evidence of the odd occurrences. You would think that with such a dedicated team and active paranormal locale the evidence would begin piling up, right? Well, not exactly. Because although everyone on the team had their share of bizarre and frightening encounters on the ranch, they proved notoriously difficult to document.

They quickly realized that there seemed to be an intelligence behind the paranormal activity – and that this intelligence was camera shy. As bizarre as it may sound, the entities were always one step ahead of the investigators and would only appear when they knew they were momentarily off guard and unable to record them!

Some might be tempted to say that the team of investigators were just a bunch of liars, but this is allegedly how things went down at the ranch. A few things were captured on film and audio but the most fantastic encounters were not. Among the more incredible things that the team allegedly witnessed were huge UFOs flying over the area, and "interdimensional doorways" suddenly appearing, which the aforementioned UFOs frequently flew through.

Team members could be sitting down on the porch of the ranch house at sunset with everything calm and in order, when suddenly what can only be described as a bright, orange portal would open up on the horizon, through which these craft would emerge. If the accounts are to be believed, these entities could manipulate the very fabric of space and time, and going in and out of these portals is an indication of just how elusive they could be. They were there one second, and the next they were not.

One of the most prevalent things the team said they encountered were objects that were variously described as orbs, balls of light, and on some occasions, clearly mechanical devices – all no bigger than a baseball – which would hover and dart around all over the property. Many were under the distinct impression that these things were some kind of drones or advanced alien probes doing reconnaissance in the area. The devices seemed to be intelligently controlled, and they, too, avoided being captured on film.

But through trickery and subterfuge the team sometimes managed to outsmart the objects and took some photos of them. Although compelling, these photos are not considered smoking-gun evidence, because even once the fast-moving objects were captured on film the images tend to be blurry and out of focus.

Bigelow ultimately disbanded his research efforts at the ranch in 2004, and the property was eventually sold to a new set of owners who are just as mysterious as Bigelow. Known as Adamantium Holdings, LLC (when it comes to aliens you should always have a limited liability company!), at the moment, nothing much is known about the company or why it is at the ranch.

But since they took over, all roads in and around the location have been cut off, ostensibly to prevent trespassing paranormal buffs from wandering onto the property. If that weren't enough, the company also has security guards posted on just about every corner of the land 24/7. It remains unclear what the newcomers have planned, but whatever it is, they are apparently taking things very seriously.

If ever you would like further information about the Skinwalker Ranch, you can read my book The Skinwalker Ranch which goes into more detail about this fascinating story.

Alien Implants

Some might scoff at the notion that alien entities would be implanting objects in human beings, but if you believe the alien abduction narrative, implants seem like the only piece of physical evidence extraterrestrials are willing to leave behind. According to the ufologists who study this stuff, in the alleged abduction program being carried out by extraterrestrials, when the aliens have abducted someone one of the first things they do is implant an object into the abductee.

The most obvious reason to do this is that the objects serve as tracking devices, so the aliens can track the victim's location no matter where they are. Many frightened abductees have claimed that they moved on several occasions, hoping to shake off their abductors, but to their horror, the abductions would continue no matter where they went.

Like an animal who has been tagged in the wild, the abductee is said to be closely monitored through the implant. But much more than simply sending out the abductee's location, the implant is also said to send important biological data to alien scientists. Some have even alleged that the implant allows the aliens to control certain aspects of human physiology. But let's discuss what solid, physical objects have actually been retrieved from people, and what testing of them has indicated.

Some of the first attempts to surgically remove alien implants were disappointing, with the alleged implants crumbling to powder or otherwise disintegrating as soon as they were removed. Some would contend that this was part of the implants' design, a way to make sure we pesky humans don't get ahold of their devices.

A breakthrough in implant retrieval was apparently conducted, however, under the auspices of the now-infamous surgeon and ufologist, Dr. Roger Leir. Dr. Leir, well aware of the stories of alleged implants self-destructing upon hitting the open air, developed a means to remove the implant while partly maintaining its environment. This meant taking some of the patient's blood ahead of time and using it as a readily available transport medium in which to place the implant.

In Dr. Leir's first attempt to remove an implant that was allegedly located in a patient's foot, it proved to be a careful "fishing expedition" to find the object in question. They cut the patient's big toe open and probed and searched for the implant. The patient was heavily sedated, but strangely, right when Leir managed to grab the implant, she howled in pain. According to Leir, the only way this would be possible is if the implant was directly connected to a nerve that the anesthesia could not reach.

Nevertheless, Leir soldiered on, and after giving her a renewed dose of anesthesia he managed to pull the implant free. According to Leir, it was a metallic object covered in a fibrous biological membrane. He said that it was triangular or even slightly T-shaped in appearance, and was small enough to fit on the tip of your finger. Before putting the object in the transport medium, Leir picked up a fresh scalpel in an attempt to cut through the tough fibrous membrane that surrounded the object.

To his shock, his blade couldn't even scratch it. The membrane was abnormally strong and impervious to his efforts. Realizing that he couldn't make any headway and afraid that the object would disintegrate, as was alleged in other accounts of implant retrieval, Leir quickly put the object inside a vial of the patient's own blood, hoping that would be enough to trick the device into thinking it was back in its designated environment – the abductee.

Many of Dr. Leir's early cases were fascinating, but the evidence was always inconclusive. There were a few objects that were tested and found to be made of rare Earth elements, and some seemed to emit electromagnetic fields or even radio frequencies, but real proof was elusive. During the course of his work, Dr. Leir would remove many of these strange objects with more or less the same result.

That is, until the good doctor came across the subject who is now infamously referred to in UFO circles as "Patient 17." Patient 17 was a man who complained of a lifelong ordeal of being regularly abducted by aliens. He spoke openly of his hatred of the insidious entities he believed to have intruded in his life and he desperately wanted an object in his leg removed. Dr. Leir operated on Patient 17 with the cameras rolling and the experienced surgeon did indeed pull a strange object out from just where Patient 17 said it would be.

Using Leir's special method of transfer so that the object would not be compromised once it was out in the open air, the alleged implant was then rushed off to a lab on the American east coast, in the state of New Hampshire. The lab results were shocking. The object was found to be absolutely loaded with iridium. What's so special about iridium? While it does exist on Earth, iridium is extremely rare and is more often found in meteorites. It is not something people come into contact with on a daily basis.

So the presence of an object made of this material found wedged in Patient 17's leg could be attributed to aliens, or perhaps he was randomly hit with a micro-meteor in the leg. Both explanations would strike those who heard them as absolutely insane, but since no one has ever claimed to have been hit by a tiny meteor in their leg, the idea that such an object was surgically inserted by an alien force seems to gain credibility.

This object was probably not of this Earth – the iridium alone is proof of that. But what else did this strange artifact do? Well, after this discovery was made things would get spooky, because when it was examined with special equipment it was found to be emitting a strong electromagnetic frequency. Was ET phoning home, or just keeping dibs on its prey?

Sadly, Patient 17 was one of Dr. Leir's last patients, since the 78-year-old passed away in 2014, shortly after completing this surgery. The UFO world is still looking for a capable surgeon to pick up where Dr. Leir left off and carry this wide-ranging investigation forward to find bona fide evidence of alien interaction with our world.

Cattle Mutilations

Cattle mutilations are some of the stranger inexplicable happenings attributed to alien activity, and they have been going on for a lot longer than most people realize. Even though in the popular imagination the phenomenon seems to have begun just a few decades ago, there are cases that go back hundreds of years.

The first case to get widespread attention in more recent times was Lady the horse. On September 9th, 1967, Berle Lewis went out to check on his beloved mare, only to come upon a horrific scene. To his shock, the horse's head and neck had been completely skinned and the body had cuts that seemed to have been made with surgical precision. Strangely, however, there was no sign of blood anywhere – either outside or inside the dead animal.

The case remained a mystery and was considered unusual enough to warrant an examination by a pathologist. That pathologist was Dr. John Altshuler, who upon examining the deceased animal was alarmed to find that the brain, spine, and several other vital organs had been removed.

Not only were they removed, but they were excised with precision he now describes as being "almost as if it had been done with a modern-day laser." Now, keep in mind that even though lasers did exist in 1967, surgical lasers did not! The only lasers available back then were big bulky machines in labs, nothing that any human would be able to haul to a farm to cut up somebody's horse or cow with.

So the mystery continued, with several weighing in on what they thought may have caused the horse's unfortunate demise. At one point, even the skeptical County Sheriff inserted himself into the conversation and claimed that the animal had simply been struck by lightning – this judgment having been made without him even coming out to see the animal. In the meantime, cattle began to turn up in similarly mutilated states.

Then, in the summer of 1973, the first alleged witness to one of the acts came forward. In May of that year, Judy Doraty, along with her daughter Cindy, her mother, and her sister-in-law, saw a UFO corner a cow in an isolated pasture outside Houston, Texas. They saw the UFO hovering over the field and then, perhaps against their better judgment, pulled to the side of the road to watch.

It is not uncommon in UFO encounters for witnesses to black out, and this is what happened. Afterward, all the women could remember was pulling to the side of the road and looking at the brightly lit UFO, and then the next thing they knew, they were driving down the road once more with no recollection of what had happened in the missing time. It was only when they consulted the famed hypnotherapist and ufologist, Dr. Leo Sprinkle, that some rather disturbing recall came to light.

Under his guided hypnotic regression, Judy would recall suddenly being inside the craft and seeing a cow being levitated up inside the vehicle's opening. She watched as it got "sucked up" into a chamber onboard the craft. To her horror, she then saw powerful lasers cut into the animal while it was still hovering in midair, the cow squirming in terror as vital organs were being removed. Various probes with tubes connected to them harpooned the poor beast and rapidly sucked out blood and other fluids from its body.

After all this, the animal was simply dropped back down to the ground, where it lay stiff, motionless, and most certainly dead. It was shortly after Judy witnessed this horror show that a couple of aliens approached her and told her that she wasn't supposed to be there. It was as if she had randomly happened upon the aliens in the middle of the act, and they were a bit surprised at the intrusion. But they then took the time to explain to her that what they were doing was necessary for the benefit of mankind.

As fantastic as this story sounds, Judy's other family members were separately hypnotized without sharing any details with each other beforehand, and each one gave an account that perfectly matched Judy's. So this was not only a witness to a cattle mutilation, but also a multiple eyewitness account of an alleged case of alien-based cattle mutilation.

As mutilated cattle continued to appear across vast expanses of the American west, Democratic senator Floyd K. Haskell decided to get involved. He used his connection with the FBI to launch a full-fledged federal inquest into the matter. To their credit, as bizarre as the case may have seemed from the outset, the FBI did indeed take it seriously.

After a thorough investigation, they would find that there had been an astonishing 8000 strange mutilation cases in Colorado alone, which amounted to over a million dollars' worth of losses to local cattle ranchers. This showed that the cases were not just bizarre, but actually hurting the state's bottom line, since that was a tremendous loss of taxable revenue.

Nevertheless, the FBI was never able to come up with a substantial resolution to the issue. And as the wave of dead cattle continued, local farmers began to take matters into their own hands, joining together with their neighbors in small bands where they would stay up late at night, shotguns in hand, just in case any intruders happened to have their cows in their sights. This resulted in farmers taking potshots at low-flying helicopters, but as far as we know, no aliens were harmed.

Although incidents of cattle mutilation have petered off considerably since the 1970s and early 1980s, they do still occur. In fact, as recently as the fall of 2019, a spate of cattle mutilations in Oregon made international news. As was reported by NPR in October of that year, five young purebred bulls mysteriously died and were "drained of blood with body parts precisely removed."

These once proud and majestic bulls were completely drained of their life force and were described as looking like deflated plush toys. They looked surprisingly fresh, with glossy fur, and remained strangely untouched by flies and parasites. But underneath the animal's pristine exterior, the bulls were missing genitals, eyes, tongue, and all their blood.

Whatever the cause may be, the slaughter of these animals is said to have amounted to a loss of over $100,000. In the aftermath, the local sheriff put up a $25,000 reward for finding the culprits. Unless someone hauls ET to the police station sometime soon, this reward money will most likely go uncollected.

Crop Circles

For some, the idea of aliens drawing doodles in a field of crops in the middle of nowhere is even more absurd than the butchering of cows that was mentioned in the previous chapter. But believe it or not, some believe crop circles might be the best evidence of alien interaction that we have to date. Theorists contend that there is much more than meets the eye with crop circles.

If aliens were to communicate with us, who's to say that they would do so by radio? What if they did so by creating geometric patterns across the landscape? If it seems odd, well, they are aliens, after all! Their methodologies would indeed be quite foreign to us. What if, for example, aliens were nonverbal?

If they didn't speak, there wouldn't be much sense in using radio for communication. Some had indeed proposed the idea that geoglyphs were an alien form of communication, but the notion really gained some traction in 2001, when a crop circle appeared in England that seemed to be a direct response to a message sent by the powerful Arecibo radio telescope some 30 years before.

The original message devised by scientists Carl Sagan and Frank Drake had basic information about Earth encoded within it. If picked up, it would have shown a primitive visual representation of our solar system, a listing of chemical elements crucial for life on Earth, the composition of our DNA, the rough population of Earth at the time, a crude stick figure sketch of a human being, and a rendering of the radio telescope that sent the message.

In 2001, a crop circle appeared that was an exact replica of the original Arecibo message, with a few crucial differences. In the so-called response, the portion listing chemical elements focused on silicon instead of carbon. The "DNA" had an extra strand inside of it, and the stick figure humanoid at the bottom presents a decidedly non-human entity – short with a large head – immediately reminiscent of the gray aliens of UFO lore. The solar system depicted is also different, ostensibly reflecting an alien star system unknown to humanity.

Many have since tried to claim that the crop circle is a hoax, but some experts have readily said it's unlikely that an average person could pull off something of this magnitude. The crop circle is so complex that most would need to practice the layout a few times in order to get it right, and no "practice runs" have been discovered.

And though it has been dismissed by critics as a hoaxer trying to get a rise out of people, as of yet, no one has come forward to claim responsibility for the crop circle.

Doug Bower and Dave Chorley have openly admitted to creating several crop circles with nothing more than a bit of rope and a plank of wood. They demonstrated how, if someone is creative and motivated enough, it is indeed entirely possible to use a plank of wood to stamp out patterns in the corn. These two are highly skilled crop circle makers and can create extremely intricate designs.

It is reported that some rather strange side effects have been recorded in the immediate vicinity of the circles. It is said, for example, that genuine crop circles tend to exude electromagnetic and even slightly radioactive frequencies. There are also subtle molecular changes to the plants which have been pressed down. We may not have all the facts yet—but some insist that crop circles are indeed proof that something otherworldly is going on.

Alien Abductions

Some understandably argue that purported alien abductions do not prove an alien presence since most cases lack direct physical evidence. But due to the huge volume of reports, the circumstantial evidence gives us enough to deserve mention. According to the testimonies gleaned from so-called abductees, the abduction phenomenon seems to have two variants.

In some cases, the event seems to be a random, once-in-a-lifetime event. Most of these cases occur when someone happened upon a UFO by chance and was taken on board the craft. The famous case of Travis Walton, the logger who was said to be accosted by a UFO in front of his entire logging crew, is of this variant. Once he was returned five days later, he never experienced another abduction.

However, the vast majority of extraterrestrial encounters seem to be part of a program with repeat visits throughout the abductee's life. These individuals appear to have been abducted, processed, and catalogued at a young age. They are said to have been implanted with special chips that track their location, monitor biological processes, and as some claim, perhaps even help to facilitate routine abduction through the manipulation of the abductee's physiology.

These repeat abductees also seem to have a family history of encounters. In many cases they find that their mother or father (or in some cases, both parents) have had similar experiences, and sometimes that their mother's and father's parents have, as well. If alien scientists are closely monitoring the development of humans, it makes perfect sense that they would closely track families in order to gauge genetic growth. That way, they would have a detailed example of how the genetics of their specimens have progressed over several generations. This is what most abductees say is happening; once an abductee is part of this program, the aliens are able to take them at will, at just about any moment. How is this done? Do the aliens knock on the abductee's door in the middle of the night?

As puzzling as it might sound at first, the most commonly reported method of extracting an abductee is by pulling them right through a wall, ceiling, or window. And when we say "pulling them through" these solid structures, we don't mean that the wall, ceiling, or window is somehow busted open in the process. On the contrary, it seems that the abductees' bodies can pass right through these solid objects.

In a typical scenario, the abductee will wake up with a start in the wee hours of the morning and feel that their entire body is vibrating. The next thing they know, they see a flash of blue light. They are sucked through what should otherwise be the solid structure of their home and transported onto the alien craft.

These are some pretty incredible stories, but is there any evidence? Sometimes, abductees have claimed that a liquid residue is left behind on objects such as windows. This material has been collected, but as is often the case with this phenomenon, it presents some anomalies but the results are inconclusive.

Without physical evidence, the next best thing to support alien abduction claims are incidents that involve multiple eyewitnesses. There are a few notable cases of this on record. One of the most potent of which is the Kelly Cahill encounter in Australia. Kelly and her husband were driving home late at night in August of 1993 when they saw what they believed to be a brightly lit blimp. On arriving home, Kelly and her husband discovered they were missing a whole hour. Kelly suffered some abdominal pains, and discovered a triangle-shaped mark near her navel. The occupants of two other cars described the same craft and the women had similar marks on their bodies.

The Allagash case is another good example. In August 1976, the four men were camping in the woods of Maine when they saw a bright, unnatural light above the trees. Two nights later, they were in a boat on a lake when they saw a similar light in the shape of a sphere hovering over the forest nearby. One of the men shone a flashlight at it, and it came toward them. They made a beeline for the shore.

The light came quite close to them but to their recollection it soon withdrew and quickly disappeared into the sky. Reaching the shore, the men hauled in their boat and went back to their campsite feeling very calm. Since they had left a large campfire burning only a short while ago, they expected it to still be going but only embers remained. Perhaps more time had passed than they thought. Feeling tired, they went straight to bed without discussing what had happened and continued their trip the next day.

Years later, the men found they were all having nightmares, and they decided to undergo hypnosis to try to determine what took place. All four men described bright lights in what seemed to be a cold hospital room, and mysterious dark humanoid figures performing procedures. Separately, they all talked about fear and feelings of being violated. Their descriptions of that night were almost identical.

As of right now, the most compelling evidence for alien abduction is the testimony of the abductees themselves. While this is not substantial enough to be definitive proof of alien visitation, it is certainly compelling enough to keep people considering the possibility.

Oumuamua

Oumuamua sailed into our solar system in 2017, and in so doing, became the first known interstellar object observed in our local stellar neighborhood. At first glance, Oumuamua may not look like much – it appears to be an elongated rock of some sort. But it's highly unusual. If it's simply a natural formation, it defies all known asteroid and comet appearances. The sum of all its oddities has led some to say that this is no ordinary space rock at all, but perhaps some sort of interstellar craft.

And believe it or not, this theory is backed up by some astronomers – Harvard astronomers, no less. Just consider the testimony of Harvard's Avi Loeb for example, who claims that Oumuamua is indeed an alien spacecraft, or at least part of one. He has put forward the theory that Oumuamua just might be a "light sail" from an advanced alien craft, one that has broken off and is now soaring of its own accord through the vastness of space.

Although humans have never built one, a light sail is a piece of technology that has been theorized by scientists here on Earth. It's one of the few ways that human beings might one day be able to travel to the stars (without breaking the laws of physics). A light sail works by aiming a high-powered laser onto a reflective surface in order to push an object at tremendous speeds – all the way up to the speed of light itself.

Such a craft, if created, could be the answer to near-lightspeed travel. Such a capability would allow us to make a trip to our nearest neighboring solar system (Alpha Centauri) in just four years, since the system is four light-years away. This is fast, considering that conventional rockets would take over 100,000 years! And Oumuamua is indeed a fast-flying object, flying faster than a normal comet or asteroid should. This speed has led

Professor Loeb to conclude that something must be pushing it from behind.

But as fast as it may be, if it were truly a light sail, it would normally be traveling much faster even than it is, so fast we might have missed its presence in the first place. This has led some to openly speculate that if it was indeed an alien craft, perhaps it was programmed to hit the brakes when it reached our solar system, and slow down just enough so the extraterrestrials who sent it could take a few snapshots and beam back the data.

Even more startling, the object was seen to pick up speed after its flyby of Earth had been achieved! Many astronomers were quick to downplay the acceleration as a quirk of gravity, but many couldn't help but wonder if it was being artificially controlled.

One of the reasons an interstellar light sail zooming in and out of our solar system like this seems so familiar to scientists on the ground is that it comes out of their own playbook. For a couple years now, plans for using a probe attached to a light sail to visit Alpha Centauri has been in the works.

Known as "Breakthrough Starshot," the plan entails sending miniature spaceships equipped with light sails to visit the rocky, Earthlike world of Proxima Centauri B. If the mission is launched and all goes well, much like Oumuamua, the craft should be able to duck down into the Alpha Centauri system, slow down long enough to take pictures and other data, and then send them back to Earth for the eager analysis of scientists. Was this also the purpose of Oumuamua? Are some unknown extraterrestrial scientists eagerly awaiting a return of data from their probe right now? We'll probably never know.

Exoplanets

Just about every month of the year there is a new headline that reads, "Most Earthlike exoplanet found yet!" And while it may seem to be merely an indication of news sites using hype to get attention, astronomers are indeed constantly finding planets that are just a little more Earthlike than the last.

But initially, "Earthlike" was a fairly vague term. In the broadest sense, Earthlike would simply mean a rocky world. So when the first rocky world, CoRoT-7b, was discovered in 2008, it was indeed described as being "Earthlike," even though its orbit was so close to its sun that its surface temperatures were estimated to reach an unfathomable 4,500 degrees Fahrenheit! This fiery inferno was also determined to have no atmosphere and is five times bigger than the Earth, so in this case, "Earthlike" simply meant it was made of rock.

Over the years, this description would continue to be selectively applied as the requirements for being Earthlike were narrowed down and further refined. By 2008, as new worlds were constantly being discovered, the designation "Earthlike" came to require that the planet in question be closer in size to Earth, and within Earth's habitable zone.

In the early 2010s, several candidates in this so-called "Goldilocks Zone" were discovered, one of the most famous being an entire system of worlds known as the Gliese planetary system. Two rocky inner planets of Gliese are of particular interest: Gliese 581a and Gliese 581b. Scientists initially thought Gliese 581c was in the Goldilocks Zone of habitability, but it was later revealed that the planet was most likely completely dry and scorching hot.

Gliese had its interesting points, but it was soon eclipsed by the even more promising Trappist planetary system, which was discovered in 2015. Revolving around a star 39.6 light-years away, the planets of the Trappist system are within their star's band of habitability, they're rocky, and they have solid cores and atmospheres. They are also believed to have water, which as far as we know is one of the main ingredients of life.

The amount of water that these planets may have is believed to be anywhere between five percent of Earth's, to as much as 200 percent, making some of the orbiting bodies true water worlds. But this was just speculation; the first time surface water was verified on an exoplanet without a shadow of a doubt came in the fall of 2019, when an exoplanet known as K2-18b was found to be covered in H_2O.

It's 111 light-years away, so even if this planet was imaged from Earth, we would be seeing it as it appeared 111 years ago. K2-18b is said to now be the best candidate for habitability that we know of right now. But having that said, K2-18b is not exactly Earth's twin.

For one thing, it's a big world – about eight times bigger than the Earth. It also orbits much closer to its parent star, but unlike our sun, this solar system's star is much cooler. This alien sun is what is called an "M dwarf," which is much smaller than our sun and nowhere near as hot. This would mean that a planet such as K2-18b being a little closer in is actually a good thing, since it would pick up extra heat that way.

The only problem with that is that it would also likely pick up more stellar radiation due to this close proximity. But if scientists know one thing about life, it's that it always finds a way to adapt. And if there is life on this alien world, it is most likely well adapted for survival. And it's possible that the planet could have a much thicker ozone layer than Earth, which would provide protective shielding for the occupants.

Being in the midst of such heavy radiation, however, would make leaving such a world much more challenging for any extraterrestrial explorers who might live there. Also, the fact that this world is bigger would make launching a rocket off the surface that much harder, since the pull of gravity would be greater.

But once again, where there is life, there is a way, and right now an exoplanet over 100 light years away by the name of K2-18b just might harbor that life. Evidence of aliens? Perhaps further analysis of K2-18b will let us find out.

Unexplained Disappearances

Have you ever heard the expression that someone simply "disappeared off the face of the Earth?" We don't normally mean that literally, but there have been unexplained disappearances that can make one wonder if this might not actually be the case. And let's say alien abduction accounts are real, isn't it possible that the aliens to keep some of those they abduct?

Sure, most of the abductee fish are thrown back, but perhaps some perish during the ordeal. Others may be detained for reasons we don't understand. If you talk to any alleged abductee, they will tell you they were afraid they might never be returned – and some say they were threatened that they wouldn't be returned if they didn't cooperate. Perhaps this was just an empty threat to get their wards to comply, but it's an alarming thought all the same.

There are missing persons cases on this planet that make absolutely no sense whatsoever. Surely some people met with foul play and others had accidents that were never discovered. Other people may not wish to be found. But what about those who go missing from their beds in the dead of night, or on the way home from the grocery store?

Then there's the case of Frederic Valentich, a young Australian pilot who went missing after reporting a UFO. He not only disappeared into thin air – he disappeared in midair! He was on a routine training mission in a single-engine Cessna aircraft. Back at mission control all was quiet until Valentich came on the line to report that he was being followed by an unknown aircraft.

He said the craft was huge, lit up like a Christmas tree, and hovering about 1000 feet over his head. He was asked to further describe the object. Valentich dutifully reported, "It's approaching from due east towards me. It seems to be playing some sort of game... flying at a speed I can't estimate. It's not an aircraft...it's...it's flying past. It's a long shape. I cannot identify more than that... It's coming for me right now!"

As the young man grew more and more panicked, he suddenly broke in, "It seems to be stationary. I'm orbiting and the thing is orbiting on top of me. It has a green light and a sort of metallic light on the outside." Valentich then expressed concern that his plane was "rough idling." After a pause, he then shouted into the radio, "It's not an aircraft!!"

That was the last anyone ever heard from Valentich. The fact that Valentich was in the process of reporting a UFO when he disappeared would inevitably raise more than a few eyebrows. But many alternative explanations have been offered to explain how he may have disappeared. Some say that he became disoriented and his craft angled sideways or even flipped upside down. If this were the case, it would be possible that the object he saw was merely the lights and shadow of his own plane reflecting upon the water. This would also explain his rough idle as he lost altitude just before crashing into the waves.

But what it does not explain is why no one ever found his body or any wreckage. Immediately after the young man's disappearance, an extensive dragnet was placed around the area as investigators sifted and searched every nook and cranny for a sign of a plane crash. But not one single piece of the plane (or Valentich) was ever found.

In the aftermath of his disappearance, some asserted that the whole thing was a prank. You see, Valentich was known to have an interest in UFOs so some (including some of his own friends) wondered if he was pulling some kind of stunt, staging his own disappearance. This is unlikely since we've been waiting now for over 40 years for Valentich to step out of the shadows and share a laugh.

Valentich isn't the only one who has disappeared under such odd circumstances. A very similar incident happened to an American Air Force pilot by the name of Felix Moncla several years before – except in his case, the whole thing was clearly documented on radar with astonished onlookers back at the base seeing his little blip on the radar screen getting swallowed up by, and become one, with the larger blip of the UFO he was chasing. This, of course, doesn't mean that the UFO literally ate Moncla's craft, but many have speculated that this was probably an indication that the UFO had somehow seized control of Moncla's jet fighter and pulled it inside the UFO's lower deck.

Perhaps an astonished Moncla was pulled up by tractor beam into the very craft he was chasing, and greeted by extraterrestrials who decided it would be best not to return him. Whatever the case may be, just like Valentich, both he and his plane disappeared without a trace while encountering a UFO.

The next case of a truly mysterious disappearance occurred at one of the most mysterious sites of all: Stonehenge. It happened in the hippie heyday of 1971, when it was a popular place for young people to hang out, sometimes camping all night in the circle. But on this particular night, the good times would come to an abrupt end. Allegedly witnessed by a local farmer and policeman who were standing nearby, a bolt of lighting struck the stones, creating a strange illumination all around the circle. The next thing they knew, there was a brief but intense moment while the campers were screaming before all suddenly went quiet. The two men ran over to see what they could do, but they found no one – only burned camping equipment.

Five young people went missing that night. While there were no direct reports of a UFO nearby at the time, Stonehenge is certainly associated with them. Some speculate that Stonehenge was created as a kind of portal to alien worlds. If this is the case, did those Stonehenge hippies get awarded an unexpected one-way trip?

A more recent mysterious disappearance that has gotten the whole world talking is that of the infamously ill-fated MH370. This large passenger plane was flying from Kuala Lumpur International Airport in Malaysia on its way to China when it vanished without a trace. It remains one of the biggest aviation mysteries of all times.

If aliens are real, and supposing they're interested in learning more about Earth's inhabitants, just think about how easy it would be for them to get specimens to study. With the technology to remain hidden and evade notice or capture, they can come and go as they please.

It's an uncomfortable thought, but it's entirely possible that some of our unexplained disappearances have their cause in alien abductions. Unfortunately, this leaves us with no proof.

The Tunguska Incident

Many are familiar with the story of the crash of an alleged alien spacecraft in Roswell, New Mexico. But what about Tunguska, Siberia? Something very mysterious occurred there that remains unexplained to this day.

In the early morning hours of June 30th, 1908, a tremendous explosion rocked the cold region. The blast was so tremendous that it leveled 1000 square miles of forest.

Fortunately for humanity, this event occurred on a desolate piece of terrain in the middle of Russia's frozen north, far from any cities. If the same explosion had occurred near a city, the devastation would have been equivalent to a nuclear bomb. Tunguska is remote, and though the area is said to have been home to tribes of nomadic hunters who perished, this has not been confirmed. Most of the world didn't seem to know that this tremendous blast had occurred until several years after the fact.

Nevertheless, it was later discovered that some of the indigenous people who lived in Russia's northernmost villages had indeed witnessed something extraordinary that day. They described a huge fireball streaking across the sky. Seconds later, there was a tremendous explosion.

Even at a great distance, the explosion was powerful enough to knock people off their feet. Some even had the windows of their homes blown out from the force. Those who were close enough felt a searing heat on their skin. But because they were a people who kept to themselves, these accounts did not spread far at the time.

The resulting fire burned bright enough to light the night sky as far away as London, and the ripples of the blast were registered as far away as Asia and the United States.

But because the area was so remote, it wasn't until 1927 that a team of Soviet scientists (led by researcher Leonid Kulik) made it to the site of the rumored explosion to investigate what had occurred. It had been nearly 20 years since the incident, and yet when this team finally made it to the remote region, they could clearly see a blast site of tremendous proportions. In this desolate wasteland, trees were flattened like toothpicks, for as far as the eye could see.

There was no sign of life. All was dead, destroyed, and ruined – laid to waste by some mysterious force. What happened? The stunned Soviets had a very hard time answering this question. The most obvious cause would be a meteor, comet, or asteroid. But there were problems with this theory.

For one, there is no point of impact that most space rock sites would have, no evidence of the spot where a space rock could have hit the ground. At Tunguska, everything seems to be uniformly flattened over a huge radius and there is no crater. And though they scoured the entire area, not one piece of a meteor, comet, or asteroid was anywhere to be found.

More recently, it has been theorized that a nearby lake called "Cheko" might have actually been created by the object, but in 2016 this theory was debunked when Russian geologists drained the lake and took sediment samples. The samples indicated that the lake was nearly 300 years old. This means it was there long before the Tunguska event occurred. So we have a huge blast site, but the normal signs of it being an asteroid, meteor, or comet are not there.

What else could it have been? After the nuclear age began with the atomic bombings of Hiroshima and Nagasaki in 1945, many began to speculate that the site at Tunguska looked much more like the aftermath of those two bombed cities than it does any meteor strike. The similarity in footage of the flattened sections of Hiroshima and Nagasaki when compared to Tunguska is striking, but as mentioned, humanity didn't have access to nuclear weapons until 1945 – Tunguska occurred in 1908.

Some speculate that the explosion at Tunguska was not a natural event, nor was it caused by humans. Why would anyone say such a thing?

First, let's take a look at the original reports given by the Siberian inhabitants, because there is one shocking aspect of their story that has not always been reported. Several witnesses claimed that the "fireball" they witnessed streaking across the sky actually began to change course. Neither meteors, asteroids, or comets would be able to change direction.

Additionally, trace amounts of radiation have allegedly been detected near where the epicenter of the blast would have occurred. This would then lend credence to the idea of a nuclear event, but it doesn't make sense. Why would an entity with the power to attack us with nuclear weapons then detonate in a remote area? This is why some Russian scientists have made the bold claim that the blast wasn't caused by a nuclear bomb, but rather a nuclear-powered spacecraft. It may even have been trying to avoid human-dense areas.

One of the more recent proponents of this theory is a Russian researcher by the name of Yuri Lavbin. Mr. Lavbin has been quite vocal about the extraterrestrial hypothesis, and he believes that just such a craft crashed in the remote reaches of Siberia in 1908, leading to the Tunguska event. He also claims that he has wreckage from this crash! His evidence was a 50-kilogram chunk of metal.

As usual in the case of UFOs, the material Lavbin recovered remains unidentifiable and tests on it are inconclusive. Some have rightfully pointed out that wreckage from Russian space flights dropping down in the area would be just as plausible a source for space debris. The jury is still out on whether Mr. Lavbin's claims are fact or fiction.

The UFO idea for Tunguska seems to have been inspired, at least in part, from sheer fantasy in the first place. It was a Russian science fiction writer who first wrote up a tale on this theme in 1946 in his book, *A Visitor from Outer Space*. At any rate, the truth is often stranger than fiction. Whatever anyone might believe, the Tunguska incident continues to be one of the greatest mysteries of our time.

If ever you would like further information about the Tunguska incident, you can read my book Tunguska – An Apocalyptic Event Beyond Belief which goes into more detail about this captivating story.

Disclosure or Disinformation? (You Blink and You Miss It!)

For decades now, those who follow the UFO phenomenon and are convinced that the government knows more than it tells us have been crying out for a little something they call "disclosure." They long for an official briefing by the U.S. government in which it comes clean about its alleged dealings with UFOs – and maybe even extraterrestrials themselves.

There have been times that the government seemed tantalizingly close to just such a revelation. Famed film director Bob Emenegger claims he was almost involved in just such an attempt. Mr. Emenegger is adamant that the U.S. government enlisted him in what they claimed at the time was a plan to make a tell-all documentary about official knowledge of extraterrestrial visitors.

Bob's story begins in the early 1970s, during the first term of the Richard Nixon administration. Nixon, despite his bitter enemies, was doing well with the average American. The economy was good, Apollo astronauts had successfully landed on the moon, the Vietnam war was winding down, and the Nixon team had just pulled off a successful diplomatic coup with China, establishing a trade partnership with the previously isolated communist nation that (albeit with its ups and downs) carries on to this day.

It's hard to fathom it in light of the Watergate scandal and Nixon's ultimate resignation during his second term, but his first term was a great success. Even so, as his first term drew to a close, the Nixon team wanted to seal the deal with the American public. According to Bob Emenegger, it was in this spirit that the idea of a "very special documentary" was concocted that would enshrine the U.S. – and in particular, the Nixon administration – as being the leaders of the free world.

Initially, Emenegger had little clue as to what kind of content this documentary touting the "exceptionalism of America" would be about. Emenegger almost declined because he had a bit too much on his plate already. But after discussing the matter with his wife, he finally agreed to at least see what it was all about. He said he would meet with the "Committee to Re-Elect the President," otherwise known as "CRP," to discuss the project. Shortly thereafter, he spoke with committee officials in California, where he was told very little about the subject matter of the documentary, other than it covered cutting-edge U.S. technology and advanced scientific projects.

Committee members believed that something showcasing American ingenuity, in much the same vein as the recent Apollo landings, would help to stir up American pride – and support for Richard Nixon's reelection. Although the details were still unclear, Bob Emenegger, who was always intrigued by the prospect of cutting-edge science, was finally convinced to participate.

Initially, there was no mention of UFOs whatsoever. Emenegger was simply told that he would be given access to select research facilities and military bases in order to document some of the more advanced projects being sanctioned by the U.S. military. After this briefing, Emenegger was then taken out to Wright-Patterson Air Force Base in Dayton, Ohio, where he was shown a demonstration in the latest in the application of laser technology.

The laser had been in experimental use since the 1960s, and while such things were indeed interesting, they were by no means earth-shattering, or even very thought-provoking. The other research projects he was shown were even more mundane;

for instance, he was taken to a base in Georgia to watch the instruction of special reconnaissance dogs. One can only imagine what might have been going through Emenegger's mind at this point.

Were they putting him on? This was the great revelation to the American people? A bunch of dogs running around looking for stuff? At this point, Emenegger must have been thinking the whole thing was a farce, but soon he would be presented with the real subject matter of the documentary. Shortly thereafter, he was taken to Norton Air Force Base and put inside a secure, soundproof room his handlers referred to as a "clean room" and was finally told just what kind of material he would be covering.

He was debriefed by an Air Force officer named Paul Shartle who proceeded to give him top-secret info on what the government knew about UFOs. With a straight face, the officer told Emenegger that both UFOs and their occupants were real. He admitted that a vast majority of sightings were bunk, but from previous investigations, the Air Force knew conclusively that a small percentage were indeed the result of extraterrestrial visitation. Shartle informed Emenegger that the matter at the moment was highly classified; however, it had been determined that some of the details would be released to the public in the form of a documentary.

Was Emenegger bearing witness to the ultimate disclosure that aliens were real? Emenegger sat in silence, stunned at what he was hearing from the decorated military man seated in front of him.

The officer proceeded to tell him that not only were the alien visitors real, but the U.S. government had established official contact with them, including an incident in 1964 in which a UFO escorted by U.S. jet fighters landed at Holloman Airforce Base.

According to the officer, this entire event was on film, showing the landing of the craft, the exiting of the occupants, and the extraterrestrials' interaction with Air Force personnel on the ground.

According to Officer Shartle, there were certain sequences from this footage that the government wished to include in the documentary. The Holloman footage was envisioned to be the stunning ending to the piece, with this monumental moment of disclosure documented for the world to see, right before the credits of the film began to roll. It was then that Shartle quickly advised Emenegger to keep the true contents of the documentary secret, as certain members of the government were not privy to this planned disclosure.

According to Shartle, this disclosure was being planned by one faction of the government and to prevent it from being shut down, others needed to be kept out of the loop. Emenegger was told that it was for this reason that he was initially sent to more mundane projects, in order to trick these other factions into thinking that such safe topics were what the documentary was to be about, and not UFOs. According to Shartle, naysayers in high places were being kept in the dark about the real production, and it needed to stay that way until the documentary was finished.

Emenegger was stunned. He had just been told aliens were real, that the U.S. government had established official contact, and that there was deep disagreement in the government over whether to share this information with the rest of the human race.

What kind of strange *Alice in Wonderland* world had he just slipped into? After this revelation, Emenegger and company were then ushered into the Pentagon, where they met with Colonel William Coleman. After introductions were made, Coleman issued very much the same warning about warring factions as Shartle did. Coleman informed Emenegger that there were high-ranking officials who supported disclosure, but there were others who would have no part of it.

He then went into detail about his own personal experience with UFOs. According to Coleman, he had a direct encounter with one of the craft as a pilot, and the experience had a profound impact on him. Coleman knew just how shocking irrefutable evidence of the existence of aliens could be.

After a general discussion of the project, Coleman then directed Emenegger to meet up with Colonel George Weinbrenner of the Foreign Technology Division, back at Wright-Patterson Air Force Base. He was going back where his journey began, but this time instead of being shown a laser light show, he would be shown something altogether different. He was tasked with interviewing Air Force officers and gathering their direct testimony of their experiences with UFOs.

But to Emenegger's shock, right at the last minute, the plug was pulled on most of the project. It seemed that the bureaucrats Coleman and Shartle had warned him about had gotten wind of the project. In the end, a compromise was made and the documentary would indeed go forward – but the revelatory footage of the UFO landing at Holloman Air Force base would not be shown.

It was deemed that the public was just not ready for such disclosure. Instead of being able to drop this bombshell of irrefutable proof of alien life on the American public, Emenegger was instead directed to create a fictionalized cartoon sequence of Air Force officials greeting landed aliens and to have the narrator read from a script in which a vague statement was made, stating,

"This is what may happen in the future...or perhaps this event has already occurred."

The finished product was called "UFOs, Past, Present, and Future," and it was vague, leaving just enough room to satisfy those who did not want to believe, and for those in government who did not want to tell, to wriggle their way out of disclosing anything substantial. You can still see this documentary on YouTube (it's variously titled "UFOs: Past, Present, and Future" and "UFOs: It Has Begun").

And even though it's ultimately inconclusive (just like every other UFO documentary), it still holds some fascinating testimony. We only have Emenegger's word to go on that there was ever meant to be something more explosive revealed.

But at the same time, Emenegger can't help but wonder if, in fact, he was the victim of a government-sanctioned hoax. In other words, was this push toward disclosure actually a massive disinformation campaign?

It certainly wouldn't be the first time the government used UFOs to cover up their own secret projects. During test flights of the top secret U2, R71 Blackbird, and Stealth Fighters, belief in UFOs was actually encouraged as a cover for these then-secret craft.

If a citizen reported seeing one in the skies, it was convenient for the military if the public turned its attention to UFOs and came up with theories to explain what was seen. So Emenegger still isn't sure if he was a dupe, and used in an elaborate disinformation campaign.

More recently, an unexpected UFO investigator – Tom Delonge, the frontman of the rock band Blink 182 – has come to the stage. Delonge has had a long fascination with UFOs and in recent

years has used his money and his prestige to forge his own private UFO research group called "To the Stars Academy," or "TTSA" for short. They began to collect metals and artifacts said to be of alien origin.
This group has managed to cobble together a network of government, intelligence, and military insiders who are dedicated to getting to the bottom of some of the most inexplicable mysteries of all time. One of the big players in this group is a former Pentagon staffer by the name of Luis Elizondo.

Elizondo was a part of the Pentagon's "Advanced Aerial Threat Initiative" that came to light in 2017. In a move that stunned the UFO community, the government admitted it had been actively investigating UFOs from 2007 to 2012, spending 22 million dollars during the enterprise. Soon after this revelation, footage was released of Navy pilots chasing down bizarre craft, complete with astonished, off-the-cuff pilot reactions such as "What the hell is that?" and "Look at this thing, dude!"

But even more astonishing was the fact that the Pentagon came out and announced that the objects in the footage were indeed real, and they had no idea what they were. In other words, without coming right out and saying that the craft captured on official military footage are aliens', the U.S. military has heavily implied that this is indeed what they are.

Perhaps the most amazing thing about this soft form of disclosure is that most of the world didn't even take notice. The information was leaked right around the holidays of 2017, when people were more consumed with their personal lives than any events on the world stage, and it seems that only those with a deep interest in the topic even bothered to pay attention.

There were brief stories on the explosive findings on mainstream news, but they were quickly forgotten without much of a ruckus at all. If this was a step toward disclosure, those in government who stressed that the American public could handle it without panicking must have felt vindicated. Because the American public not only handled it, most simply ignored it.

At any rate, it was after this revelatory news was released that Luis Elizondo resigned from his post, stating that he felt the government needed to divulge even more information. It was a short time after leaving the Pentagon that Elizondo hooked up with Tom Delonge and TTSA. With TTSA, Delonge created a virtual dragnet that scoured the globe in search of evidence for extraterrestrials.

In these efforts, no stone was left unturned to uncover footage of alleged UFOs or fragments of alleged extraterrestrial craft. Things seemed to have come to a head in September of 2019, when TTSA came into the possession of a video taken by Navy personnel of a craft that was referred to as the "Gimbal." Shockingly, this move prompted the U.S. government, for the first time in recorded history, to confirm that the footage taken sometime in 2015 was indeed an authentic, unexplained event.

The U.S. military and government officials had long gone to great pains to extricate themselves from the business of saying what was a UFO and what was not, but here they were, going on the record and directly confirming that a craft seen darting around on video wasn't a hoax, wasn't swamp gas, wasn't a weather balloon – but a bona fide UFO!

Even as they made this confirmation, officials warned that such classified material should not be released. But in October of 2019, shortly after Tom Delonge and company released the Gimbal footage, the bizarre announcement was made that the U.S. Army was going to directly partner with TTSA!

The reason? Well, do you remember those UFO fragments and unidentified alloys that Delonge's group had been collecting? Well the U.S. Army is apparently interested in utilizing them to enhance their ground forces. The U.S. Army has officially partnered with a former member of a punk rock band to back-engineer alleged alien alloys from extraterrestrial craft! In official statements, the U.S. Army has stated that it intends to use what they have termed "exotic material" to create next-generation weapons and defense systems for ground vehicles such as enhanced camouflage, "inertial mass reduction," and unspecified aspects of "quantum communication." The long-awaited disclosure of UFO lore now seems to be upon us, and with today's instant news cycle moving at the speed of light, it's all happening so fast. If you blink, you just might miss it!

It's All in the Eye of the Beholder

Are aliens real? Well, in many ways it always seems to depend on whom you ask and how they perceive the alleged evidence of an alien presence on Earth. For some, many of the accounts in this book would seem to present an overwhelming indication that there is something to the UFO/ET phenomenon. For others who are not quite so comfortable with the idea, however, there is almost always a way out of this conclusion.

Just take the recent revelations of the Pentagon's UFO investigation program – one of the most startling alleged evidences of extraterrestrial visitation – which is in the process of rapidly unfolding as of the writing of this book. The implications seem incredible, but even this alleged proof has a possible exit for those who would rather have this particular conspiratorial maze *not lead to aliens* at the end of it.

Because as damning as some of this may seem, in the end it could be just another shell game of disinformation. What if those alleged alien alloys were actually pieces of a top-secret American craft? The U.S. government of course would not want to blow their cover and admit as much, so maybe just to shut Tom Delonge and his cohorts up, they play the game of pretending it's aliens.

The same could go for some of the more startling footage and encounters experienced by Navy pilots. If this were next generation advanced military craft that only the top echelons of the military industrial complex were aware of, those in the know would have to lie to much of their own personnel about its existence. And when called into question, pointing to UFOs would be an effective way to do so.

As you can see, in the convoluted world of the UFO/ET phenomenon, sometimes even instances that appear to be clear-cut evidence, may in fact be something else entirely.

On the other hand, if the government had compelling physical evidence of extraterrestrial visitation, one way to kill the public's interest in it might be to release flimsy, false evidence and accounts that wouldn't fool the average person. As we've seen time and time again, and as people who formerly worked high in the government have said, somebody knows something.

The trouble is that what we can seek as concrete evidence seems limited to physical pieces of spacecraft and video of non-human entities, both of which could be faked well enough to fool the average person. Events like cattle mutilations and unexplained disappearances – even suspicious asteroids – can't be proven one way or another, as suspicious as they are. Does the sum total of ufology's claims add up enough that we can comfortably say there's something to all this? Many think so.

None of this addresses the uncomfortable fact that, if an alien race had the power to get here in the first place, they most likely have the means or technology to go undetected. Even humans now have the technology to modify DNA and create new kinds of life, and a sudden physical takeover of the planet isn't the only way aliens might arrive.

We can't prove they've been here, but we'd have a heck of a time trying to prove they haven't.

Further Readings

Now that we have reached the end of this book, let's take the time to go over some further reading and reference material. Here you will find complete sources of information covering all of the topics presented here. Feel free to browse through them all.

The Presidents and UFO's: Secret History from FDR to Obama. Larry Holcombe

This book provides a rather fascinating read about alleged presidential involvement with the UFO phenomenon. One of the most shocking claims is leveled by film director Robert Emnegger who relates a tale of being tasked with making a documentary for official government disclosure. It is important to note that none of his claims have been proven. But having that said, Mr. Emnegger is a respected professional who has stood firm behind his account to this very day.

The Alien and the Scalpel. Dr. Roger Lier

In this book, the late great Dr. Roger Leir walks us through his strange world of implant removal. Leir spent many years as the only known surgeon to actually claim to have removed artifacts from an alien civilization. Lier would pass away in 2014, leaving behind a treasure trove of information. This book covers a large chunk of his work and make for a fascinating read.

Hair of the Alien: DNA and Other Forensic Evidence for Alien Abductions. Bill Chalker

Here in this book, Bill takes us down the road of alien evidence in the form of an alleged encounter an Australian man by the name of Peter Khoury had in the early 1990s. Bill keeps his narratives to the point and presents compelling data as to the unusualness of his findings. An excellent resource for those looking for the closest thing to evidence that can be found in regard to this phenomenon.

Above Top Secret: Uncover the Mysteries of the Digital Age. Jim Marrs

Here in this book, Jim Marrs lays plain some of the strangest aspects of many things that we hold dear. In his quest of unraveling unimagined mysteries, he even takes a stab at the moon. It was from this book that much of the lunar conspiracy theories presented in this book was gleaned. Mr. Marrs was an expert on all thing's conspiracy and this book most certainly does not disappoint.

Divine Encounters: A Guide to Visions, Angels, and other Emissaries. Zecharia Sitchin

Sitchin is another great researcher/writing in the field that is no longer with us, but during his lifetime he uncovered more than most. An expert on ancient Sumerian script, it is from Sitchin that much of the strangeness of ancient Mesopotamia has come to life. His books are a must read for anyone wishing to learn more about ancient astronaut theory.

The Day After Roswell. Philip Corso

Here in this book, a retired military professional by the name of Philip Corso gives what amounts to a deathbed confession. Relating the monumental task that he was given in assembling a team to back engineer technology recovered after the Roswell crash. Whether you believe it or not—it's a fascinating read.

Also by Conrad Bauer

Printed in Great Britain
by Amazon